Exploring Life's Perspective Through Poetry

Karla Culbertson

BookLeaf Publishing

India | USA | UK

Exploring Life's Perspective Through Poetry
© 2024 Karla Culbertson

All rights reserved.

No part of this publication may be reproduced, stored in a retrieval system, or transmitted, in any form or by any means, electronic, mechanical, photocopying, recording or otherwise, without the prior written permission of the presenters.

Karla Culbertson asserts the moral right to be identified as author of this work.

Presentation by *BookLeaf Publishing*

Web: www.bookleafpub.com

E-mail: info@bookleafpub.com

ISBN: 9789363305960

First edition 2024

This book is dedicated to everyone who has ever believed in my abilities as a writer and furthermore, my passion to become the best poet that I can possibly be and become.

Footprints

If I were to follow your footprints on the sand
It would take me away to a heavenly land
Once I approached you you would gently take
my hand
And we would sit together on the sand
Enjoying one another's company and gazing into
each other's eyes
Promising to love one another until the day that
we die
Promising to take each other's faults and see
them as human
Instead of mistakes
To treasure each other every day

No matter what may come our way

"Union"

Union is to come together
Joined together by love
Even when it is falsified
By the majority
Because of differences
Even though that is what makes us human
To keep going no matter what all of the
disbelievers say
It is a feat on its own
To stand up for yourself
When everyone else expects you to shut down
Is a new kind of heroism

Attitude

An attitude is a collection of thoughts
That is meant to be complex
Just like the human spirit
Sometimes we may shift our attitudes
As a way to fit in
Especially when we are teens and want to fit in
To that special mold that we see as accepted
The one that will score you some friends
And more importantly popularity
As we grow older and mature
We tend to see the world in a new light
We begin to love ourselves as we are
And as we realize what we did to have an
acceptable place in the world
We know that it does nothing but leave behind a
scar
One that may never heal
But then that is when we realize how important
it is to be real

Charity

I am the type of person who sees people who
give back
As a masterful work of art
Charity should be displayed and looked at with a
keen eye
You never know where the loyalty will lie
But you hope that there will still be some
recognition
You hope that one day you will see the kind of
treatment you deserve
On the world's bigger stage
But for that to happen there must be significant
change

Silence

For many years there has been so much I want to
say
So much that has opened my eyes
It is often found that I have a very different
opinion from the majority
Something that could cause discourse and throw
kindness off-track
So I just reinforced my tact
And stay immersed in the silence
I know that it's not healthy
But if I am loud
I know everyone would be ready and willing to
tear me down
The silence can be dark
But I know one day when I am ready to emerge
I will make my mark

Uneven Pavements

These uneven pavements

I walk along

It seems to be going so wrong

A bit like hearing the same song

All day long

When things go right

I try to embrace who you are

But you still seem distant

Out of my line of sight

I reach for you

But suddenly you jerk away

I see you sway

And I see her smile

And suddenly you feel so far

Something like a Million miles

Between you and me

Two lost souls

Who have similar goals

The grief seems to swallow me whole

I miss you and the days of old

Hold me Closer

The distance between us

Leaves me with a guilty feeling every time

I want to kiss your lips

Hold you close at the hips

As we twist and dip

I have always imagined a man

Like you in my dreams

I want to get lost in your eyes

To explore your thighs

Hold me closer and hug me tightly

Wrap your body around mine

And know that life can change

On a dime

Once upon a time

You were the person whom I have

Always dreamed of

Broken Record

As the evening fades into the night

My soul seems to come alive

I will do just about anything to provide

I want to see you thrive

And grateful to be alive

I know that your life feels like

A broken record

The bad things stalling on repeat

Skipping over the hard times

And trying to understand

Why this keeps happening

Over and over like a carrousel with no brakes

I feel dizzy

From throwing myself into a tizzy

I just want to be happy

To feel the love and be sappy

Midnight

The glow from the moon pierces my eyes

I look up there wishing I could see you

To bathe in the moonlight

And love life like I always thought you could

Separating bad from good

Evil from angelic

You were always fantastic at reading people

And could tell me how they felt

Before I even recognized it

I imagine you are dancing at midnight

Fully embracing your time in heaven

Floating high above the clouds

Lavish Life

I grew up thinking that I wanted a lavish life

You always want what you don't have

And what you cannot imagine grasping

You grew up grappling with the problems of the poor

You never imagined you'd have much more

You did not think you could accomplish much

Given where you have come from

But how wrong were you?

You have sprung forward

With so much advice to give

That is as valuable as the sunshine

And as predictable as the rain

You have done all of it

While you have worked to maintain

What was soon to be yours

In Abundance

All at once

And without the cushion of a lavish life

Hollow Heart

When I first married you

It seemed like you couldn't get enough

Of me and my body

But as soon as we had kids

Something changed

It seems you vanished

Like a ghost in the night

Vanishing like a wizard performing

Its latest magic trick

You just slipped through my hands

Like nothing else mattered

Your hollow heart dancing in the background

Like a treasured mannequin

Rainbow

This continuous rain

Has caused a flood

And has left me feeling trapped

Within myself

Feels like my spirit is

Dripping with fear and stress

All my possessions

Now consumed in water

Soggy and depressing

Waiting for the rainbow to appear

A sign of 'peace and content

I like to think that the array of colors

Would somehow positively influence me

Somehow brightening my spirit

In this time of doom

Love needs some room

In my heart

To Hold You

To hold you is like being trapped in paradise
forever

To hold you is never something I plan to take
advantage of

To hold you is a dream come true

Something I never thought I'd be able to do

Going from lost to complete was a bit of a
mystery to me

Once I got used to the routine

I began to truly realize what a blessing it was
meant to be

That is not to say the storms were not heavy

Just like everyone else we had our
disagreements

There have been times when our tempers have
flared

Like the wind in a hurricane

But we refused to let it tear us apart

That is how I know our marriage starts with the
heart

To hold you is like being trapped in paradise
forever

To hold you is never something I plan to take
advantage of

To hold you is a dream come true

Something I never thought I'd be able to do

Going from lost to complete was a bit of a
mystery to me

Once I got used to the routine
I began to truly realize what a blessing it was
meant to be

That is not to say the storms were not heavy

Just like everyone else we had our
disagreements

There have been times when our tempers have
flared

Like the wind in a hurricane

But we refused to let it tear us apart

That is how I know our marriage starts with the
heart

Lost

I waited so long to feel complete

It felt like a marathon that never ends

It was worth it at the end of the day

All of the exhausting days

And those in between

You make me feel as though I was just seventeen

You were my everlasting ray of sunshine

I was so glad that you had chosen to be mine

But now that you're gone

I feel like a first-time driver

Missing directions

Even when the answer is right in front of me

I could go on forever about how unfair life can
be

But what good would it do?

It would not help me fill the empty space

So, I will continue to take my time

One of these days I will find my rhyme

And understand the reasoning

It is just a matter of a healthy balance

And as long as I have the patience

I know that will come to me in time

Flowers

I still remember when we got married

The day is still so clear in my mind

Giving the memories of the best time

We were surrounded by the prettiest flowers

Each one delicate in its own way

Like the sunrise and sunsets

Our parents took so much of their time

And money to make it the most perfect day

There is something so special about such a gesture

It will never tire or age in my mind

Like a fine wine

Storybook

Once upon a time
When you were mine
Our love was like a storybook
It was as if my biggest dream had finally come
true
I would pledge to give you my love and stand by
your side
No matter how dark the time
No matter how bright the day
My love for you is here to stay

Rhyme and Reason

Please give me a rhyme and a reason
Why you're here to pick up the pieces
I do not know what I did to deserve
All of this sweet love you are here to serve
Whatever the reason
I remain grateful for this season

Twist and Turns

Among all of the twists and turns
There is a lesson here to learn
It sends me into a tizzy
It makes my mind so dizzy
I will never understand
Why you refuse to miss me
I did all that I could
Your wish was my command
I went to grab your hand
And you quickly turned away
I may never know
What caused our relationship to sway
I would do just about anything
If you'd be willing to understand
I want what we used to have
To come soaring back
But in the meantime, I will continue to pick up
the slack

Love

Your love is so pillowy and soft
A safe place to land
When life feels unkind
If we could turn back time
I would go back to the day
That you asked to be mine
It felt so perfect and serene
The kind of thing you only see
In a movie scene
My eyes filled up with tears
For I had been imagining
This kind of love
For so many years
The way you look at me
With such pride
Makes me await the day
That you ask me to become your bride

Dance

You make me want to throw up my hands and
dance
For you put my mind into a certain trance
The first time I saw you
I knew that I would be captivated by your beauty
You shine from the inside out
You turn my doubt into truth
You are my solid proof
That love is not a spoof
But something to be taken seriously
And treated with the utmost delicacy
So let's turn up the music and dance the night
away
And cheers to living life the right way

The Beginning

Take me back to the start
When life was new and free
When you could open up and bloom
Without worrying about running out of room
There was so such thing as doom
All of the happiness in the world
Just waiting for us both
Sometimes life is not always what it seems
It is all about learning to spread your wings

www.ingramcontent.com/pod-product-compliance
Lightning Source LLC
LaVergne TN
LVHW041253200726
843507LV00013B/2954